The Earth Dwellers:

Revelation as Revolt

Joey Nelson

ISBN-10:1463770049
ISBN-13:978-1463770044

DEDICATION

To you Babe. Thanks for making my life possible. I want to love you well, as you have loved me. You are incredible and amazing.

To you kids. I want to have those who know me the best to love and respect me the most. I love being with you and always will.

To you readers. I want to see you go further than you ever have before in one of the most exciting books in history – the Book of Revelation. Keep growing!

To the Lion Lamb. Always Your Follower. Forever In Your Grace. May you Reign Forever!

UPCOMING BOOKS[1]

The Lion Lamb: Revelation as War

The Saints: Revelation as Journey

The Dragon: Revelation as Fantasy

The Demonic Locusts: Revelation as Horror

The Worshippers: Revelation as Multi-Dimension

The Sea and Land Beasts: Revelation as Politics and Religion

The Chosen Lady: Revelation as Biography and History

The Harlot: Revelation as Eroticism

The Bride: Revelation as Love Story

The Throne Sitter: Revelation as Theology

The City Dweller: Revelation as Comedy

---

[1] This is not necessarily the order in which the books will be published.

CONTENTS

ACKNOWLEDGMENTS

I would like to express my gratitude to Stone's Hill Community Church, Ligonier, IN. You were the first to receive this series of talks on the Book of Revelation. And now, we get to share it with the world. Thank you for your support, your feedback, and your love.

INTRODUCTION

> *"Aim at heaven, and you will get earth thrown in; aim at earth, and you will get neither."*[2]
>
> C. S. Lewis

The Earth Dwellers: Revelation as Revolt is the beginning of my personal journey through a Bible book that I have been reading and studying for over twenty years. One does not just haphazardly read, dissect and chart this book and thus have it mastered. There is way too much going on in the text for that kind of approach.

Quite honestly, I have been somewhat reserved about speaking and writing on the Book of Revelation. It has taken me a long period of time to read and ruminate on all that is here. While I will never feel that I have totally mastered this material, I feel that the time has come to share with others what I am seeing in one of the most fascinating books in the Bible.

The Major Characters Tell the Story Best

John, the author, apparently exiled by the Roman state on an Island named Patmos in the Aegean Sea, wanted to connect many of the key prophetic passages that are in the Old Testament into a roughly chronological framework that would help enlighten all readers of things to come. John pulls together several strands of prophetic thought from several books in the Old Testament. But he does not present this information in a boring or sterile way. Instead, John weaved all of this information into an exciting, powerful, and highly visual story with stunning characters in a great plot. That is what I want to focus on in this series of books. The major characters

---

[2] Lewis, C. S., *The Joyful Christian*, (New York: Macmillen, 1996), pp. 118-119.

tell the story best. If we understand them, we understand the story.[3]

The Character of "Earth Dweller" To Begin This Series of Books[4]

I begin this series of books with *The Earth Dwellers* for at least three reasons.

First, this character in particular holds an interpretational key. If we understand the underlying themes of rebellion and revolt on the part of human beings in this story, then we understand why a Lion Lamb (Jesus Christ) had to be sacrificed and why the Throne Sitter (God) decided in heavenly places to win us back. Revelation teaches us that there is something wrong in the world –that our hearts are messed up. It teaches us that the Throne Sitter refuses to let us go our own way without endeavoring to woo us to Himself at great personal cost through personal engagement in our world.

Second, Revelation teaches us that God honors human free will to the very end, and that, therefore, our decisions really do matter. It is important to get this early in the book. Humans in revolt against the Throne Sitter barricade themselves in, in order to keep God out. And this rebellion plays out in Revelation.

---

[3] *The Earth Dwellers: Revelation as Revolt* (and all subsequent books in this series) will work off of the premise that Revelation is a chronological arrangement of events. However, John interjects supplementary material into the chronological flow of events (these will be dealt with in upcoming books). There may be *flashbacks* of things that John has already covered and there may be *previews* of things to come. But the story moves forward in terms of time. See Appendix One.

[4] See Appendix Two for a list of the major characters that are found in Revelation. This will be a character driven series of books, but the character studies will be situated within the chronological framework John presented.

Third, most people question how just and fair God really is for allowing the things found in Revelation to happen to human beings. If it can be demonstrated that the rebellion of free will human beings is one of the key reasons we have the book of Revelation, then all the other things that happen in this book can be clarified and understood. If we as humans know what our role or potential role may be in this book (depending on what our decisions are), then our responses to all the other things we learn from the characters in this book can begin to be shaped earlier in the drama. Revelation is meant to challenge who and what we are loyal too. John argues for complete loyalty to the Lion Lamb. This study will get to that issue more quickly than in the explanation of any other character. And, if we know that the actions of God are justified in how He handles Himself in Revelation, then our resistance to His truth can be lessened and we can get more out of the studies to come. In a way, this first book in this series demonstrates that God not only holds the world accountable for centuries of accumulated rebellion, but He also works with humanity over time, in order to bring them back into relationship with Himself.

Revelation is a sensational, vivid description of things to come in the last days. It is God's final word or story to man. Revelation is considered by many to be "apocalyptic" literature. That is, it addresses or "uncovers" issues related to the end of the current age. It uncovers things to come, but it is organized along the lines of an engaging story. *The Earth Dwellers* (and all books that follow) will serve to simplify this final and great story by looking at the major characters within the story and the role they play as human history winds its way to conclusion in preparation for a new age.

1 THE OVER-ARCHING STORY

Revelation is the first century literary equivalent of Blu-Ray®. It is full of color, vivid details, and literary special effects that would have grabbed the attention of any listener in the first century.[5] There are visions, places, creatures, songs, cities, and armies, all of which when described by John, leave us back on our heels. John talks about an earth that quakes and a sky that falls, about bottomless pits that hemorrhage with smoke and about a lake of fire from which there is no return. He talked about kings who ride into war, about demonic-inspired warriors who have supernatural weapons, and about those who wreak havoc on mankind. According to John, there will be natural catastrophes, supernatural interventions, and man-made tragedies as this planet rocks and reels under the accumulated burden of life in rebellion against God. And, John also talks about a man riding in on a white horse to save the day just in the nick of time. What a story!

---

[5] Some have asserted that the illiteracy rate in the first century was extremely high. This makes a book like Revelation stand out in sharp relief. People could listen to it being read and easily stay engaged with all the action and word pictures that John painted for the reader.

Revelation is a story complete with plot direction, character development, and unique settings. Undoubtedly, John was a good writer, but the weight of his visionary story even taxed and pushed his talent and vocabulary to the limits because he relied heavily on figures of speech, on simile and metaphor to get things conveyed.

A Familiar Story, Yet New

Contained within the book are the same elements, patterns, and archetypes found in some of literature's greatest stories. Literary archetypes are familiar patterns that we see in many stories. For example, John wrote about a lady who was in distress who was marvelously delivered. How many times have you seen this in a movie? (Think a large ape with sharp pointed teeth that holds a woman in his hand while atop the Empire State Building). You and I have seen a lady in distress a thousand times in the movies we have seen and the books we have read.

John also included a dramatic hero who killed a dragon. Every story must have a hero, someone that all the action happens to and through. Incidentally, the Lion Lamb hero (Jesus Christ) prevails in this book! It is really all about Him.

And every great story has to have an evil villain who is finally exposed. The counterfeit trinity of the Dragon, Anti-Christ and False Prophet are fully exposed and relegated to a place where they cannot molest creation anymore. John uses metaphor and symbolism and familiar archetypes and many powerful literary techniques as "special affects" in this first century masterpiece.

Leland Ryken, a literary expert, contends that we actually find that the last half of Revelation is "a spiritualized version of familiar archetypes." Ryken writes about:

> "a woman in distress who is marvelously delivered (Revelation 12), a hero on a white horse who kills a dragon (Revelation 19), a wicked prostitute who is finally exposed (Revelation 17), the marriage of a triumphant hero to his bride (Revelation 19), the celebration of the wedding with a feast, and the description of a palace glittering with jewels in which the hero and his bride live happily ever after (Revelation 20-22)."[6]

So John clearly wrote a story that is very familiar (we have seen this before in other stories and movies), and yet it is very new and definitely packed with theological and eschatological meaning. It is high drama, a Blu-Ray® approach, to stun the "viewer" or hearer with sights so vivid you can almost smell it.

How the Story Goes

Here is the story I get after reading the Book of Revelation. There is a Lion Lamb (Jesus Christ) who is worthy of our worship and who is qualified to accomplish what is written in the ancient scrolls (the Book of Revelation). The Throne Sitter (God) and the heavenly counsel approve of His credentials and qualifications to open, and thus place into effect, the contents of the ancient scrolls. There are Lion Lamb followers (Saints) who will be loyal to the Lion Lamb to the very end, despite the Dragon (Satan), a variety of Beasts (Land and Sea), and a sensuous Harlot that tries to draw them away. And, there are also Earth Dwellers who are in league with those who want to defeat the Lion Lamb. After an increase in natural calamities, there will be a short period when a pseudo-ruler

---

[6] Ryken, Leland, *Words of Delight: A Literary Introduction to the Bible*, (Grand Rapids: Baker Book House, 1992), pp. 488-489.

(Anti-Christ) and government will hold sway over the world and trouble those who align themselves with the Throne Sitter and the Lion Lamb during this period of time. It is very clear that signs of God's divine judgment will precede the return of Christ to planet earth (this period is usually called the Tribulational Period by Bible scholars). Those who refuse to repent are held accountable and given what they have wanted all along – life without God in it. This is followed by personal resurrection and judgment and cosmic restoration. And only One (the Lion Lamb) is worthy to see this plan through to completion. What is more, the Lion Lamb gets the girl (the Bride of Christ – the Saints) at the end of the story. The faithful Lion Lamb followers get to attend the marriage of a triumphant hero to his bride in a palace glittering with jewels in which the hero and his bride live happily ever after. Good wins over evil. The injustices of the world are made right. The results of the Fall are reversed. That's the movement – the over-arching story of John's Revelation.[7]

Why So Complicated?

While doing a series of talks on the book of Revelation, my son Levi asked, "Dad, why did John not just say things simply without all the symbolism and complicated story-line?"

"Here is at least one possible reason why," I told him. "If you are in prison or exiled on an island by the Roman Empire, they are going to be monitoring everything that you say and write. John was seen as a suspicious individual, as someone who was dangerous to Rome, a political threat, a leader of a movement that was seen as seditious. John has to write in code because the 'Roman Gestapo' we could say, could potentially find and censor his material. He talks later about the Roman Empire and her rulers (and about coming rulers), but he does so in a way that the Roman propaganda police would not know

[7] See Appendix Three for a more detailed overview.

what he meant (he references all anti-God systems as 'Babylon' in Revelation 17-18). But people (Lion Lamb followers) who were thoroughly familiar with the Bible would understand all the symbolism and Old Testament allusions that John makes in this book." Levi said it made sense.

In Nazi Germany, I have heard that captive Jewish artists in concentration camps were creating paintings and drawings that were being shipped around the world. And behind these works of art, they included other paintings or sketches that depicted what was really going on in the Holocaust. They smuggled them out by placing them behind the acceptable pictures, thus avoiding the Gestapo's censoring. The world eventually got the message.

I think that is what John is doing. He is hiding the message from those who would destroy it in order to get the word out to people living in persecution who need to know what is going to happen. I think John meant to be an encouragement to those weighed down by persecution from a Roman government that had very little patience for Lion Lamb followers. John's striking story would prompt them to hold on and endure because they know how the story is going to resolve eventually.

John is also creating a work of art. John is seeing a vision and he presents it in a way that his first century readers could relate, even though many of his readers may have been illiterate. Hearing the story was their primary means of learning and the visuals that John creates ensured that the story would be heard, paid attention to, and would be remembered and passed on. A story like John told, not only cements itself in our memory, but it makes us think about where our own loyalties are. It makes us reconsider our own priorities. It makes us think about what we need to do in order to align ourselves with the Lion Lamb.

Yet, even so, John also wrote about a constituency of people who refuse to follow the Throne Sitter and the Lion Lamb. John talked about a group of people that he references as "inhabitants of the earth" or we could call them "Earth Dwellers" who refuse to give the Throne Sitter or the Lion Lamb their place.

2 THE EARTH DWELLERS

There are three predominant images in Revelation according to a book by Paul Spilsbury.[8] Those images are: the Throne, the Lamb, and the Dragon. In the Throne, we have One who has all power and authority (note the interspersed throne scenes – Revelation 4-5; 7; 11; 15). In the Lamb, we have One who was slain and who is worthy to open the judgments of this book (note the focus on blood - Rev. 1; 5; 7; 12; 13; 17). And this Lamb is the King over all creation. In the Dragon, we have a beast who is seeking to sabotage a good creation by organizing the empires of the world (code named "Babylon") against the Lamb using all means possible – religion, politics, academics, and social interests (Rev. 12). As powerful as the Throne Dweller is, and as loving and sacrificial as the Lion Lamb is, according to John's story, there are some who will side with the rebellion led by the Dragon Beast (Satan himself).

What Is An Earth Dweller?

John called those who side with the Dragon the "inhabitants of the earth" or Earth Dwellers (Revelation 6:10). This group

---

[8] Spilsbury, Paul, *The Throne, The Lamb & The Dragon: A Readers Guide to the Book of Revelation*, (Downers Grove, Illinois: InterVarsity Press, 2002).

of people refuse to repent, or change their mind, about who they will give their allegiance to.

When I was writing this book, my son Will saw the rough draft and commented that he thought the title of the book was weird. We do not normally think of humans as "Earth Dwellers". Yet, the more I think about it, the more I see John's point. Earth Dwellers are those who live only for the earth. They only live for what they see, for the things they can possess for the power they can weld, or for the prestige they can accumulate. And, they persist in these beliefs over an entire life-time on earth. John said that they are mere Earth Dwellers, living only for the now.

Despite the cycles of judgment that grow more intense on earth (something we will look more closely at in chapter three), instead of softening their hearts in response to the unspeakable calamity going on in the world, they steadfastly harden their hearts and refuse to change. No matter how bad things become in Revelation, Earth Dwellers refuse to repent during the unfolding of these cataclysmic events. Inspired by the Dragon Beast (Satan) and his minions, Earth Dwellers refuse to give God His place in this great drama. They live to revolt.

John wrote in Revelation 6:10:

> "They called out in a loud voice, 'How long, Sovereign Lord, holy and true, until you judge *the inhabitants of the earth* and avenge our blood?'"

Those Lion Lamb followers who have been swallowed by the Dragon's wrath cry out for justice toward the "inhabitants of the earth" or Earth Dwellers.

What John Says About Earth Dwellers

Earth Dwellers are actually mentioned in several places in Revelation. Earth Dwellers rejoice when the two witnesses are killed in Revelation 11:10:

> "The *inhabitants of the earth* will gloat over them and will celebrate by sending each other gifts, because these two prophets had tormented those who live on the earth."

These two witnesses proclaim God's plan for the world and the Earth Dwellers celebrate to have them removed.

Earth Dwellers worship the beast. In Revelation 13:8:

> "All *inhabitants of the earth* will worship the beast—all whose names have not been written in the book of life belonging to the Lamb that was slain from the creation of the world."

And in Revelation 13:12:

> "He exercised all the authority of the first beast on his behalf, and made *the earth and its inhabitants* worship the first beast, whose fatal wound had been healed."

The beast represents a vast anti-God kingdom that convinces all Earth Dwellers to buy into his world domination.

Earth Dwellers are drunk with the harlot's wine in Revelation 17:2:

> "With her the kings of the earth committed adultery and *the inhabitants of*

> *the earth* were intoxicated with the wine of her adulteries."

The use of religion and politics is referenced as a Harlot that people do adultery with, especially Earth Dwellers.

Earth Dwellers are subject to the coming hour of trial in Revelation 3:10:

> "Since you have kept my command to endure patiently, I will also keep you from the hour of trial that is going to come upon *the whole world* to test those who *live on the earth*."

And in Revelation 8:13:

> "As I watched, I heard an eagle that was flying in midair call out in a loud voice: 'Woe! Woe! Woe to *the inhabitants of the earth*, because of the trumpet blasts about to be sounded by the other three angels!'"

Earth Dwellers will drink the cup of God's wrath, not because they have to, but because they chose to drink it.

There are some who have so given themselves to pure evil that they will never turn back. Their hearts have been hardened. No matter how bad things are, they still rebel against God, and the judgments keep coming.

In Revelation 9:20-21, John wrote:

> "The *rest of mankind* that were not killed by these plagues still did not repent of the work of their hands; they did not

> stop worshiping demons, and idols of gold, silver, bronze, stone and wood—idols that cannot see or hear or walk. Nor did they repent of their murders, their magic arts, their sexual immorality or their thefts."

And in Revelation 16:8-9, John once again wrote:

> "The fourth angel poured out his bowl on the sun, and the sun was given power to scorch people with fire. They were seared by the intense heat and they cursed the name of God, who had control over these plagues, but they [Earth Dwellers][9] refused to repent and glorify him."

Earth Dwellers and the Book of Life

Earth Dweller's names are not written in the book of life in Revelation 17:8:

> "The *inhabitants of the earth* whose names have not been written in the book of life from the creation of the world will be astonished when they see the beast, because he once was, now is not, and yet will come."

Earth Dwellers will be drawn into following the Dragon's program and will not be detoured in doing all that he prompts them to do. In Christ, Lion Lamb followers names' can be written in the Book of Life. But if we reject Him and align

[9] Brackets are mine.

ourselves with the Dragon, it is as if we eliminate our name from the Book.

In conjunction with Revelation 17:8, I want you to note Revelation 3:5 which is written to the Church of Sardis and balances out Revelation 17:8:

> "He who overcomes will, like them, be dressed in white. *I will never blot out* his name from the book of life, but will acknowledge his name before my Father and his angels."

This seems to suggests that everyone's name (all of humanity) has been written in the Book of Life. There is inclusion before there is exclusion hinted at in this verse. But, depending on your free will and the decisions you make, you have the capacity to get your name blotted out of this book.

Because of Christ, your name has been written in the Book of Life. In Christ, all have been redeemed, forgiven, and saved. But if you reject God and refuse to entertain Him in your knowledge and life, then you in effect declare that you do not want His covering or provision. You do not want your name written in a Book of Life. You have your own book and you will write the story the way you want to. If that is the attitude of your heart, you are not an over-comer as Revelation defines it. You are a worshipper of the Dragon and the Beast; you are an Earth Dweller who lives only for the now, the shallow, the vain, and the temporary. And what God does in Revelation is just reaffirm the decisions that you have already made. He allows you to go in the trajectory that you want to go and He will never force you to side with Him.

Revelation makes it clear, that not everyone will be saved. Some will choose separation from God, barricading themselves in to keep God out. They will consent to the blotting out of their name from this Life Book. But if you give your life over to the Lion-Lamb who was slain by divine plan eons ago in order to rescue a fallen humanity, your name stands in the record. It is not blotted out. It has been written and it stays written in the Book of Life.

The Earth Dweller in All of Us

Quite honestly, there is an "Earth Dweller" in all of us. We have all gone our own way, lived only for the now. We have pursued earth's riches to the exclusion of eternal things. We have resisted the Throne Sitter and have ruled from our own thrones.

Some time ago, I posted a note on my Facebook© page. I had written it during a time when I was feeling especially introspective. I saw my hurts, hang-ups, and heart issues with brutal honesty. There are times in my life that I do not follow the Lion Lamb to the degree that I need to. So feeling confessional and somewhat safe in my journaling, I wrote these words based on the beatitudes in Matthew 5:

> "Instead of poor in spirit, I'm often looking forward to the next exciting thing in life rather than just facing that I can't handle life in my own strength. I'll just distract myself from my truest, deepest needs and the One who can meet them. Instead of mourning and dealing with the aches of life, I sidestep the hard places and difficult emotions… . I want to numb the pain rather than process through it. Instead of being meek and content and submitting to God's authority and His plan for meeting my needs, I met my needs my way. I live for the next thing – the next weekend, the next job, the next adventure, the next

> thrill. I hunger and thirst for all the wrong things and try to fill my life with them. Rather than take my soul cravings to God, I take them to other things and end up feeding on spiritual junk food. I can be harsh with those who live under my own roof and deny them grace. I can get really ticked at people who pretend and pose, especially when it comes to the spiritual life. They won't admit anything and pretend to have it altogether. I don't want to show them any mercy. My heart is often divided among misdirected priorities. A pure heart is an undivided heart – a heart that is no longer struggling to decide where it will give its loyalty. Rather than making peace, it's often easier to settle just for what makes me happy. When push comes to shove, it's much easier to take the path of least resistance and blend in. My name is Joey and I am a believer in Jesus Christ who struggles with just about everything that Jesus asked me to do."

There, I finally got it said and I feel better just to own that. So, when I write about Earth Dwellers, I do so with a humble recognition that there is an Earth Dweller, not just in you or in others, but in me. However, I am resolved to wean myself off of my "Earth Dwelling" ways and to pursue the Lion Lamb and trust in His grace. And if the truth be known, perhaps that is the primary reason why I wrote this book – to see the Earth Dweller in me and rely on the Lion Lamb to shape me into a fully surrendered follower.

3 A WORLD IN TRANSITION

John is portraying a world in transition in Revelation. Human history will eventually give way to a new Kingdom age according to John. One age will get swallowed by another and the book of Revelation records what that transition will look like. The world will go through a period of *uncreation* as God prepares to *recreate* all things new.

Taken as a whole, Revelation 6 is one of the most pivotal chapters in the entire book. As I worked through Revelation 6-16, it left me feeling breathless, doubled-over and gasping for air. This section of the book is not for the faint of heart. It is deeply disturbing.

Revelation 6 begins "the Day of the Lord"[10] time period, so often talked about in the Major and Minor Prophets of the Old

[10] This is a special phrase used by the Biblical writers to describe a season of time (not just a 24 hour day) when God will hold the world accountable for their rebellion. See Zechariah 14:1; Joel 1:15; 2:1, 11, 31; 3:14; Malachi 4:5; 2 Peter 3:10-13.

Testament. It is heavy on military-type descriptions of what will happen, with graphic comments of destruction, of blood-shed, of cosmic catastrophes (a key phrase that stands out in my mind from this section is "the winepress of God's wrath").

Judgment With Enduring Results

Revelation 6 begins to describe the three main cycles of judgment in the book of Revelation (known as the seal, trumpet and bowl judgments). Each judgment cycle introduces events that will have ongoing results. And with each additional cycle of judgment, the affects are combined and intensified, and they fall with drop hammer rapidity, affecting more and more Earth Dwellers. The seal judgments impact a quarter of the earth. Revelation 6:8 says:

> "They were given power over *a fourth* of the earth to kill by sword, famine and plague, and by the wild beasts of the earth."

The trumpet judgments impact a third of the earth's population after it has already been reduced by twenty-five percent from the previous cycle of judgment. Revelation 8:7 says:

> "A *third* of the earth was burned up, a third of the trees were burned up, and all the green grass was burned up."

The bowl judgments seem to affect the whole world. In Revelation 16:8-9 we read:

> "The fourth angel poured out his bowl on the sun, and the *sun* [which impacts the entire earth][11] was given power to

[11] Brackets are mine.

> scorch people with fire. They were seared by the intense heat and they cursed the name of God, who had control over these plagues, but they refused to repent and glorify him."

With each new judgment, the overall effect will be intensified until planet earth is reeling and rocking under the culmination of all these things.

To remind them, Revelation 6 is an overture that strikes all the themes that are to come and emphasizes the inescapability of it all. By the time we get to the final judgments in Revelation 16, things are moving at breakneck speed. These judgments gradually move to global proportions, as the story progresses to a finale, from a quarter of earth's population being impacted in the seal judgments, to a third in the trumpet judgments, to the whole earth in the bowl judgments. And all three judgment cycles end with a storm-earthquake. It's absolutely breath-taking.

It Really Is About Grace

You might be thinking "How cruel?" But I'm thinking "How gracious?" God fires warning shots – from a quarter, to a third, to the whole and still Earth Dwellers refuse to repent. They ignore the breaking sound of the seal judgments. In subsequent chapters following Revelation 6, Earth Dwellers turn a deaf ear to the trumpet judgments. And they blatantly disregard the bowls of wrath. God sends these "attention-getters" in order to woo belligerent rebellious humankind into reconsidering their destructive path. God sends reminders before He sends judgment. He is so gracious. After insuring that this planet, this giant spaceship called earth, has worked consistently and faithfully millennium-after-millennium, how could humans possibly have issues with seven years in Revelation? God's grace has been immeasurably great.

But Earth Dwellers will not change. This continued lack of repentance through these cycles of judgment is evidently one of the central reasons why the judgments keep coming. When human rebellion and God-hatred reaches its fullest measure, then Revelation 6 and following is what we have. There will come a time when the people of earth will use the earth to barricade themselves in so as to keep God out. God grants them what they want temporarily – a world without a God that holds it altogether. Again, the purpose of these judgments is to warn people about the fullness of judgment to come and to encourage Earth Dwellers to repent. God started with a quarter. He moved to a third. He eventually encompasses the entire world because rebellion has moved to global proportions.

This all seems to portray a world in transition, a vivid portrayal of how human history and government will terminate and eventually give way to a new Kingdom age. One age will get swallowed by another and Revelation records what that transition will look like. If we likened it to birth, Revelation is the birth pangs of a new age being born. And once this transition starts, much like birth, it will happen quickly, with several successive catastrophic events that build with intensity.

Words of Assurance

When we read about judgment and world catastrophe, it tends to alarm us to the point of fear. We wonder about survival, about our families, about health, about food. We truly do fear the unknown. John seemed to anticipate this and offered assuring words to Lion Lamb followers. Earth Dwellers are subject to the coming hour of trial in Revelation 3:10. However, Lion Lamb followers will not be:

> "Since you have kept my command to endure patiently, *I will also keep you from the hour of trial* that is going to come upon *the*

> *whole world* to test those who *live on the earth*."

Though events go global, the Lion Lamb will keep or protect those who follow Him.

4 GLAD TO BE LEFT BEHIND

Some authors, such as Tim LaHaye and Jerry Jenkins have popularized the teaching that the Church (Lion Lamb followers) will be raptured (snatched away) prior to the main cycles of judgment in Revelation (Revelation 6 and following). This indeed could be the case.[12] But, what I do not see in Revelation is a group of people agonizing and fretting over being "left behind" because they missed the rapture. I would like to think that Earth Dwellers would eventually say in response to the cycles of judgment, "Oh my, we have messed up here. We missed it. Let's change", and thus turn to God. But their attitude will be much more resistant based on the profile that emerges in Revelation. It will be more like "Hooray, good riddance. Those Lion Lamb followers have been a thorn under our saddle for centuries. Now we can run the world our way. This earth is ours."

---

[12] Many authors contend for a Pre-Tribulation Rapture of the Church, which means that the church saints will be caught away out of the world before the Tribulation begins. A solid argument can be made for this position. But I will not deal with this issue in this book. It will be given a full treatment in books to come.

That response is what I sense in John's story. We read about Earth Dwellers who have to drink the "cup of God's wrath" in Revelation (14:10). But what I sense is that their attitude is not, "Oh please do not make me drink that stuff. Oh please, please, please, do not make me." No, in Revelation, it is more about Earth Dwellers who will say, "Give it to me you Bastard Deity. I'll drink it despite you and your Cross and your cosmic sadistic ways!"

I do not see people who want into heaven, but yet, are not allowed to enter. What I see in Revelation is that Earth Dwellers are like "I do not want inside your heaven. I do not want to be with you or your kind for eternity. Give me the earth only and leave me alone."

Earth Dwellers are rebel fugitives on the run from God. John states in Revelation 6:15:

> "Then the kings of the earth, the princes, the generals, the rich, the mighty, and every slave and every free man hid in caves and among the rocks of the mountains."

So rebellious are Earth Dwellers, that they will seek escape in death rather than avail themselves of God's grace via repentance. They will not call out to God. They can find salvation in the Lion Lamb. But look at who, or I should say "what" they call out to; they call out to nature.

Revelation 6:16 says:

> "They called to the mountains and the rocks, 'Fall on us and hide us from the face of him who sits on the throne and from the wrath of the Lamb!'"

Earth Dwellers have reached a stage in life, where it is not so much that they cannot repent; it is that they will not repent. Even crying out for death in this manner is an expression of rebellion. They are determined to be successful rebels to the very end.

This rebellion is beyond just the problem of evil, the issue of pain, a detached intellectualism, or scientifically-influenced doubt. It is more about, "I will not give God His place. Refusing to believe in Him and love Him is my way of getting back at a God I detest so much and who let things go wrong in my life and in our world. I don't believe in God, but I do believe in man. And we are not going to be subject to any deity. Who is with me?"

Revelation records the story of successful rebels to the very end. It's not so much about evidence for God as it is people wanting revenge for God supposedly placing them in this mess. Earth Dwellers want to live their lives as they wish and do not want any god interfering with it. The problem is that it was God that gave them life to begin with, but that is something that they do not seem to see. They are, in fact, glad to be "left behind".

Left Behind, But Loved

Something else needs to be said here. In talking about Earth Dwellers and their animosity toward the Throne Sitter and Lion Lamb, one might be inclined to think that Earth Dwellers are the reason for all the world's problems. But I feel I need to check this thinking. Earth Dwellers are the people that God calls us to love. They might be glad to be left behind, but Lion Lamb followers are to share their love and discover the stories of those who seem so far from their true home.

From Earth Dweller to Lion Lamb Follower

I have sampled many different authors and noticed many different styles of writing, but I admit that I am drawn to honest voices like Donald Miller, Ken Gire, Brennan Manning, Anne Lamott and others. The books that I find myself gravitating to the most are those that are written by authors who are totally honest – no posing or faking, authors who unmask and become real while they share their message.

In the Spring of 1984, Ann Lamott was pregnant from a relationship with a married man.[13] She had an abortion. She tried to push away the sadness with pain pills, washing them down with alcohol, drinking through the night, through the darkness and the loneliness and the pain. Night after night, she continued this ritual of remorse. By the seventh night, she was hemorrhaging profusely. After a long night, the bleeding finally stopped and she crawled back into bed, frightened and alone and disgusted with herself. As she lay there, a strange sense of someone else's presence came over her. She turned on the light. Nothing. Her suddenly sober eyes searched the room. Still nothing. Finally, she turned off the light. After a while, the presence returned. This time she knew who it was. It was Jesus, the one John called the Lion Lamb in the Book of Revelation. She felt him sitting in her bedroom loft, hunched in the corner, kind of like a "cat". She wrote about it: "I was appalled. I thought about my life and my brilliant hilarious progressive friends. I thought about what everyone would think of me if I became a Christian, and it seemed an utterly impossible thing that simply could not be allowed to happen. I turned to the wall and said out loud, 'I would rather die.'"[14] Jesus said nothing in reply. He just sat in the corner, watching her with patience and love. This experience haunted her. She tried to dismiss it. After all, she had not actually seen or heard anything. "I mean, it

[13] Lamott, Anne, *Traveling Mercies: Some Thoughts on Faith*, (New York: Anchor Books, 1999), pp. 48-50.

[14] Ibid, 49.

could have been guilt-induced, or alcohol induced," she thought.

The next Sunday, she went to the church she had been visiting. She was too hungover to even stand. The preachers' words seemed ridiculous to her. "But the closing song felt like something was rocking me, holding me like a scared kid, and I opened up to that feeling – and it washed over me." Anne slipped out of the service, weeping as she ran. All the while she felt the presence of that little "cat", running after her. By the time she came to her houseboat, she stopped at the door, stood there a minute, then hung her head, blurted out an expletive, then sighed: "I quit." She took a deep breath and said: "All right. You can come in." And that, as she put it, "was my beautiful moment of conversion (with help from Ken Gire in retelling Anne's story[15])."

Telling the story of getting real with God does not require that we become street-corner preachers and convert people by concussion, one Bible-sledgehammer blow after another. It simply means we share with others who we truly are, how we truly need Jesus, and how Jesus is bringing us into new life and catching us up in a story. The cry of our generation is for people to be real and to lead authentic lives. This is how Earth Dwellers can be loved.

---

[15] Gire, Ken, *Divine Embrace*, (Carol Stream, Illinois: Tyndale House Publishers, Inc., 2004), pp. 182-185.

5 A REFRAIN OF UNREPENTANCE

The events of Revelation 16 occur very close to the time of the second coming of the Lion Lamb. The judgments described happen in rapid succession. By the time the Earth Dwellers reach Revelation 16, they have had seven seals and seven trumpets. In the final series of seven (seven bowls), world events will crescendo into the second coming of the Lion Lamb in Revelation 19. After Revelation 16, (John includes supplementary material in Revelation 17-18), Earth Dwellers witness the breaking in of a Lion Lamb Kingdom. Rebellion will have run its total course. Man's rebellion will be complete. God's Kingdom will invade this planet, even though a contingency of people have barricaded themselves in to keep God out. What is so astounding, is even after these cycles of judgment, we read in Revelation 16:9:

> "They were seared by the intense heat and they cursed the name of God, who had control over these plagues, but they refused to repent and glorify him."

They curse God and talked bad about him and this becomes their refrain of unrepentance in Revelation 16 (see verses 9, 11, 21 below in that order).

> "They were seared by the intense heat and they cursed the name of God, who had control over these plagues, but *they refused to repent and glorify him.*"
>
> "and cursed the God of heaven because of their pains and their sores, but *they refused to repent* of what they had done."
>
> "from the sky huge hailstones, each weighing about a hundred pounds, fell on people. And *they cursed God* on account of the plague of hail, because the plague was so terrible."

As mentioned earlier, if Earth Dwellers miss what some call the "rapture", their response will be "Good riddance. We didn't need the loser Lion Lamb followers anyway." If these people have to drink the cup of God's wrath, their response will be "Give it to me you Bastard Deity. I will drink it despite you!" The Earth Dwellers persist in their rebellion. Inspired and greatly influenced by this time by demonic-presence, they will refuse to repent.

"I Will Not Bow"

Even though I have not covered all of the biblical real estate in this first book of this series, allow me to reflect on all that has been experienced by Earth Dwellers by the time we reach the end of Revelation. Looking over John's story, it is evident that Earth Dwellers have witnessed the supernatural preservation of the Lion Lamb followers through all the judgments of Revelation. Earth Dwellers have witnessed the seven seals, the four horsemen, the rise of the blasphemous anti-Christ, the war, the famine, the collapsing cosmos, the earthquakes, the heavenly disasters, the disease, the plagues, and the enormous loss of life. They have witnessed the one-hundred and forty-four thousand (Jewish evangelists) and their message and their supernatural preservation. They have witnessed the demonic locusts and may have even been afflicted by them. They have witnessed the dynamic-duo take on the beast and win against Him for three and one-half years as they shared the love story that God has been trying to tell humanity all along. They have witnessed countless martyrdoms where Lion-Lamb followers laid down their lives for the Lamb. They have witnessed the Dragon, Satan, pursue with anti-Semitic fervor, the chosen people of God, Israel. They have watched as the kingdom of the Beast grew out into every aspect of life and controlled the world. They have witnessed the counterfeit trinity manipulate Earth Dwellers into receiving the "mark of the Beast." They have witnessed an Angel proclaiming the "eternal gospel."

Revelation 14:6 says:

> "Then I saw another angel flying in midair, and he had the *eternal gospel* to proclaim to *those who live on the earth* [Earth Dwellers][16]— to every nation, tribe, language and people."

Slow down for a moment. Is this saying what I think it is saying? That Earth Dwellers will have an angel preaching the gospel to them? These four terms (nation, tribe, language, people) stacked against each other signify universality. The "eternal gospel" includes a comprehensive message for all Earth Dwellers. This is the only time that "gospel" appears in this book. The gospel is a message of total restoration. Evil is

---

[16] Brackets are mine.

vanquished. Righteousness prevails. People are rescued. God does it for all. So it's Good News in as much as it lets everyone clearly know what is going on and what they can do about it and what God has done about us. If somehow you missed hearing the messengers of God clearly in the Tribulational judgments of Revelation, an angel will once more lay it out very clearly. Imagine, an angel telling Earth Dwellers exactly what is happening while exhorting them to change their allegiance from the Beast to the Lamb. But still, they refuse?

Earth Dwellers have even been scorched by the sun. It is like they are possessed and are no longer rational human beings. And still, they repent not and their rebellion plays out. In fact, they just curse more.

Revelation 16:21 says:

> "From the sky huge hailstones of about a hundred pounds each fell upon men. And they cursed God on account of the plague of hail, because the plague was so terrible."

If you manage to survive the quake underneath you in Revelation, you may not survive the hailstones above you. Whatever is still standing in Revelation 16 will be smitten with 100 pound chunks of ice screaming out of the earth's atmosphere at blazing speeds. Nothing will be left. God purges and cleanses the earth of everything that defiles it. And Earth Dwellers once again will be defiant, "Bring it on you monster, you idiot, you loser. You missed me on that one!"

A Successful Rebel in a Failed Rebellion

In Revelation 17-18, Earth Dwellers witness the collapse of the vast kingdom of the Anti-Christ. The 666 (the counterfeit trinity – the Dragon, which is Satan; the Sea Beast, which is the Anti-Christ; and the Land Beast which is the False Prophet) –

the 666 has been confronted with 777 (the 3 cycles of 7 judgments each) and the disintegration has begun. Earth Dwellers see the military's of the world gather for battle. Their decision has been made despite God giving them opportunity after opportunity to know what was coming and to call on Him and His Lion-Lamb for salvation. Tragically, they no longer are responsive to God's invitations to sacred romance.

6 DAY IN COURT

Many Earth Dwellers will lose their lives prior to the great final judgment of Revelation 20. But, in Revelation 20, Earth Dwellers are raised for a final day of reckoning. Now bear in mind. They have existed in hell for a period of time in some form, experiencing separation from God. However, even this has not changed their refrain of unrepentance. Amazing. I have met (and parented ☺), self-willed and obstinate people. But I have never seen anything like this. They take revolt to a new level.

The Throne Sitters Court

Revelation 20:12 reads:

> "And I saw the dead, great and small…"

Earth Dwellers come from all walks of life. Some are great rebels and let the world know it. Others are quiet rebels and serve in churches. The great rebel will be confronted and the small rebel, who thinks his or her rebellion is not that significant, will stand before God.

Revelation 20:12 continues:

> "...standing before the throne."

They are in a standing posture to receive their sentence. And they are no longer dead physically (they are able to "stand"); but they are dead spiritually in unbelief. The purpose of this judgment is not to determine who goes to heaven and who does not. It is to demonstrate how and why those who go into the lake of fire have actually chosen this destination over and over again in their lives.

> "...And books were opened. Another book was opened, which is the book of life. The dead were judged according to what they had done as recorded in the books."

This judgment will be a judgment of all unbelievers (all Earth Dwellers) of all time. It is a courtroom scene, yet it is unique. There is a Judge, but no jury. There is a Prosecutor, but no defender. There is a sentence, but no appeals. This is clearly God's court. This is the Throne Sitters court and He metes out judgment perfectly. There are multiple books so that a double check can be made to insure accuracy.

All of our stuff is kept in God's great library. The books are first century symbols for the record of every life and judgment based on that record. Sadly, Earth Dwellers have chosen to opt their name out of the book of life long, long ago. When they were born, their names were written there. But as they lived their lives, they persisted in their rebellion. They did not want God in their lives anymore. The record of their rebellion now stands. Their deeds have been recorded. All the times that God in grace reached out to them have been duly noted with their responses. The books are checked, cross referenced, and double-checked.

Searching For Any Evidence of a Repentant Heart

I think the books are checked, not just to find fault, but to find any evidence whatsoever that might indicate a repentant move by the Earth Dweller toward the Lion Lamb. I get the sense that God is looking, not just at all the times they rejected His love, but He is looking for any and every reason that somehow indicates to Him that they have this little bit of thirst for Him, the slightest inkling to want to know the Throne Sitter and the Lion Lamb and to love them would be considered. But nothing can be found that has stood in the records, even after spending time in hell. And now, in a state of rebellious non-repentance, their sentence will be pronounced.

And if these resurrected persons are consistent with what we have seen of Earth Dwellers in Revelation, then it is not so much, "Man, I hope my name is in that book. I'd give anything to have my name in that book." It is more about, "Give me the damn book! I will show you what I think of your big Book of Life. You have never run the universe right and you never will. I should be the one on the throne! You should stand before humanity and be judged! No. I will never let you put my name in your Book."

And even after careful search, if their name happened to be found, they would still be defiant: "Expunge my name from the book! I want nothing to do with this blasted God." They will be cursing God all the way to the entry point of the Lake of Fire and beyond. Their eternal legacy will be, "I will never serve you." As they are led away, yet again, I can hear their rebellion being expressed, "You Cosmic Sadist. You Hater. You Manipulator. You Dictator. No. No. No. You will never rule over my life! You are not fair. You are not just. You played favorites. You were not there for me. You did not give us enough evidence. Arrest Him. Arrest Him! He is the real criminal here! He should be standing trial here." But it will be to no avail. A good and loving God will finally give them what they have always wanted – life separate from God.

Rebels to the Very End

Earth Dwellers clearly do not want to be with God or his people under any circumstance. Their decision has been made despite God giving them opportunity after opportunity to know what was coming and to call on Him and His Son for salvation. Their hearts are so hard in fact that a solar flare cannot even melt it and hail stones cannot soften it and a stint in hell could not dissuade them. What I am sensing here is that they have reached a point of no return and while repentance is still possible, they themselves will not allow it. If Earth Dwellers have not changed by Revelation 16, they are not going to change. Their minds are made up. They are actually going to go through with this rebellion-thing. They are going to choose the Lake of Fire, successful rebels to the very end. They are going to be eternally unrepentant. They will not repent of what they have done.

7 MODERN DAY EARTH DWELLERS

Earth Dwellers are humans but they have become a Dragon-inspired, shell-of-a-person. They are shallow with a God-hatred that refuses to go away. They persist in sabotaging God's good creation. They have barricaded themselves in to keep God out. No matter how bad things get on earth, Earth Dwellers, living only for the now and the material, refuse to repent, successful rebels to the very end (Revelation 9:20-21). There is even a sense of pride that I sense in these Earth Dwelling texts of revolt. "I defied God and refused to bow" is what I hear in them. Catastrophic judgment will not even change them.

Earth Dwellers Today

Modern day Earth Dwellers live with alternative explanations for how things came into existence. They insist that the world is here to serve them. With serpent-hissing pride, they refuse to give God his place and to honor God's principles. They are determined to present God as a cosmic sadist to whom they will never bow. Men become like beasts under the Dragon's influence with the kingdoms of men, acting almost subhuman toward one another and toward God in Revelation. To deny God His place of authority over our lives allows Earth Dwellers to do wrong and call it right and even to pretend like we do not know what we really do know in our conscience.

There even comes a time in Revelation 9:5, when demonic locusts are allowed to plague Earth Dwellers for five months, possibly forcing insanity because they cannot even die.

> "They were not given power to kill them,
> but only to torture them for five months.
> And the agony they suffered was like that
> of the sting of a scorpion when it strikes
> a man."

I imagine that some Earth Dwellers will feel betrayed. They gave themselves to the Earth-Dweller cause. They made science God. They preached moral freedom and free sexual expression. They gratified their senses with any and every pleasure. They ignored their family and let their kids do anything they wanted without correction. They fought against any and every family value. They lived for the accumulation of assets to go with their other Earth-Dwelling causes. They played God. And now, what is their reward? "We're going to keep you alive a little longer just so we can watch you suffer a little more." This is the Dragon's work, inflicting pain and heart-ache. The sting of betrayal may be worse than the scorpion sting itself.

What Have We Become?

When we call abortion "liberty", euthanasia "mercy", and suicide "medicine", we can give any morally outrageous behavior a good label to justify its presence in our lives. Some have even proposed grace-periods where parents have so many days to decide if they want to keep a newborn baby. Child molestation is now called "intergenerational intimacy." Unmarried couples assert that "we do not need promises because we are in love." Of course, those who do need promises somehow now love imperfectly. And, is pregnancy really an illness to overcome? What have we become? We do not lack moral knowledge. We suppress it and re-label it so that we can do what we want.

J. Budziszewski has written a book called *The Revenge of Conscience.*[17] He talks about all these elaborate ways we go about suppressing the truth. Everybody who wants to get rid of God will eventually have a Godless world, a world with no moral values, a world where a suppressed conscience will wreak a kind of revenge. The soul of the nation is rotting as we rid ourselves of all boundaries and taboos. It is as if the fiery red horse of the apocalypse is already riding over this planet, "Men will slay each other," John wrote in Revelation 6:4.

Exploitation seems to be the global theme of our Earth Dwelling times. The planet is exploited and misused by big industry. Nations are exploited for their resources. Young people are exploited for their money and drug purchases. Media industries move teenage trends like pawns in a chess game to get youth culture to sell their agenda or buy their goods. Political candidates exploit Christian jargon to play to the voters. Pornography media giants exploit women and their bodies. Large corporations exploit employees and their pensions. Third-world nations exploit their citizens and deny them food and water and homes. Children are exploited for convenience and sexual favors. The poor are exploited through the lottery and gambling. Governments promise to meet social needs, but enslave the people, and even use crisis for a political agenda. Parents exploit children by selling their kids out for money. Animals are even exploited and abused for scientific reasons. Natural disasters seem to hit our headlines every week. People are exploited and leveraged for gain in so many places in our world. Women are reduced to sex objects. Men are

---

[17] Budziszewski, J, *The Revenge of Conscience: Politics and the Fall of Man*, (Dallas: Spence Publishing Company, 1999).

reduced to success objects. We consume one another. Wombs are vacuumed out so that they can be used again for our own selfish, valueless purposes.

Modern day Earth Dwellers are creating a world that will wreak its' own havoc; it will have its revenge. We need the in-breaking of a Kingdom. Evil is so intertwined into culture that it will take the cataclysmic, immediate intervention of God to deal with it. That is what Revelation is about.

Denying God His Place

Christopher Hitchens (an avowed atheist) would be considered an Earth Dweller by most people. He does not disbelieve in God because he thinks there is no evidence for it. Here is what he says regarding the existence of God:

> "And I don't want it to be the case, that there is a divine superintending celestial dictatorship from which I could never escape and that abolishes my private life…that would supervise me, keep me under surveillance in every moment of my living existence. And then, when I died, it would be like living in a heavenly North Korea where one's only duty was to continue to abase oneself and to thank forever the dear leader for everything that we are and have."[18]

Hitchens wrote a book, *God is Not Great: How Religion Poisons Everything*. What is so clear is that he does not want to believe in God. If he can caricature God into this cosmic sadist, it makes it easier for him to convince others that his rebellion is

[18] Lawrenz, Mel, *I Want to Believe: Finding Your Way in An Age of Many Faiths*, (Ventura, CA: Regal, 2007), pp. 85-86.

justified. Spoken like a true Earth Dweller. Many want to make God into a Cosmic Sadists in Revelation. But in fact, it is a merciful God working with free will creatures, some of whom deny Him His rightful place. It seems to be the only way they have of getting back at a "God" they cannot stand.

8 PHARAOH-HARD

One writer does something that is helpful. He says that many of the judgments in Revelation remind us of the plagues of Egypt, except in Revelation they are replayed with greater severity and geographical scope. "Thus we find in Revelation several references to the oceans turning to blood, not just rivers as in Exodus. Darkness, hail, boils and locusts are worldwide. At one point frogs come out of the mouths of the dragon, the beast and the false prophet (16:13)."[19]

In the Old Testament exodus account, God was confronting human arrogance and pride. Several times in the Exodus account, God is said to have hardened Pharaoh's heart (Ex. 9:12; 10:1, 20, 27; 11:10; 14:8). To harden meant *to strengthen* the resolve he had in his heart. According to Greg Boyd, what the Exodus account also shows us is that seven times the text says that Pharaoh hardened his own heart before the Lord took this action (Ex. 7:13-14, 22; 8:15, 19, 32; 9:7). A loving God tries to turn people toward himself. But when they reach a point of no return, God's strategy is simply to give them what they want.

---

[19] Spilsbury, Paul, *The Throne, The Lamb & The Dragon: A Readers Guide to the Book of Revelation*, (Downers Grove, Illinois: InterVarsity Press, 2002), p. 116.

He strengthens them, even to rise up against Him.[20] That is what we see in Revelation – human-beings with hard hearts given up to their depravity.

The ultimate wrath of God is not when God strikes a person down. It is when you are so belligerent and stubborn, that God says, "OK, have it your way." God gives you over to your beliefs or non-belief, hoping that the emptiness of it all will turn you back to Him. But again, Revelation records this stunning response by Earth Dwellers in Revelation 9:20:

> "The *rest of mankind* that were not killed by these plagues still did not repent."

To "repent" means to "change your mind." They will have sign after sign that God exists, that He is at work in the world, that He still loves. But, they will offer alternative explanations to all these things, and go on in their rebellion with a mind unchanged.

I like what Walter Elwell shares.

> "Perhaps it is troubling to read so much of God's wrath in Revelation, but four things must be remembered.
>
> First, God's wrath and judgment are not arbitrary, but are always in response to man's sin…
>
> Second, judgment comes only after other avenue has been exhausted, preliminary testings, short-term judgments – all

[20] Boyd, Greg, *Is God to Blame?*, (Downers Grove, Illinois: InterVarsity Press, 2003), p. 189.

> before the final wrath appears. [God doesn't just stomp us out in Revelation. It all plays out very methodically and even in a grace-filled manner.][21]
>
> Third, God's nature does not change in the exercise of his wrath. God is love (1 John 4:16) even when he must pass judgment upon the wayward peoples of the earth.
>
> Fourth, in all of this ample opportunity to repent is given. That people did not do this is testimony to the deep-seated nature of the human predicament and our bias toward evil."[22]

The Earth Dweller's heart is Pharaoh hard.

---

[21] My inserted comment in brackets.

[22] Elwell, Walter (Editor), *Evangelical Commentary on the Bible*, (Grand Rapids: Baker Publishing Group, 1989), p. 1220.

9 MONUMENT TO HUMAN FREE WILL

Revelation explains why Hell exists. It is a monument to human freedom. Hell has already begun for Earth Dwellers, long before they are cast into the Lake of Fire. I like C. S. Lewis here. He suggests that Hell is a kind of negation, a sort of cosmic void, lacking life in a full-bodied, robust sense. To enter Hell is to be banished from a full humanity. He says:

> "What is cast or what casts itself into Hell is not a man: it is remains."[23]

Hell is what is left over after you have consumed the earth and been consumed by your fellow Earth Dwellers. Earth Dwellers are barely whole people. They have shriveled up spiritually. Their spiritual and mental anguish centers on a repressed regret, a sense of loss, and the devastation of permanent exile from God, from truth, goodness, and all that is beautiful.

---

[23] Lewis, C. S., *The Problem of Pain*, (San Francisco: HarperOne, 2001), pp.125-126.

My Favorite C. S. Lewis Truth

According to C. S. Lewis in *The Great Divorce*, there are two kinds of people in the world. Those who say to God "Thy will be done." And those to whom God will finally say, "Thy will be done."[24] If you want life without me, you are permitted to choose it of your own free will.[25] He honors free will to the very end and the Lake of Fire is a monument to that. We are not "sent" to hell; rather we choose it.

"Over My Dead Body"

The world is in conflict and rebellion, but yet first on the field of battle is Jesus. It is over His dead body that Earth Dwellers will choose hell, but you can, despite His love. And if you do, you are choosing to walk away from His provision of protection from divine wrath. He is the slain Lamb who gives life to all.

Love Knows No Other Way

How does the message of God's love square with all this judgment? Evil and sin are parasites that feed off the good. It is like a virus or cancer. It is imbedded in everything now, even free will human beings. God has to let free will play out because that is how He made the world. Love knows no other way. But God's world is also built in such a way that cause-and-effect relationships exist between evil and God's response to it. Death is not a random punishment. It is the inevitable consequence of turning against the source of all life in the

---

[24] Lewis, C. S., *The Great Divorce*, (San Francisco: Harper One, 2001), pp.72-73.

[25] There is no such thing as "God rejecting our rejection of Him." Our beliefs matter. The idea that all humans will be saved in the end (called absolute universalism) contradicts the clear teaching of Revelation. Many will choose the Lion Lamb. But there is a group called Earth Dwellers (per the thesis of this book) who will not let love win over them.

universe. Rebellion has happened and it cannot be arbitrarily taken away. Jesus had to die for it. God was the only one who could provide the solution to our evil. His divine justice burned against His only Son who absorbed our penalty. Jesus is your sin-bearing Savior who shields you from the coming days of judgment. But if you refuse God's provision, you are exposed to the time when God obliterates evil. And He does so without imposing on our free will.

Free Will Playing Out

That is what Revelation is about. That is why we even have a Revelation that plays out like it does. God is going to allow free will humans full expression of their rebellion. It is God honoring free will to the very end. Otherwise, He could be like a guy with a magnifying glass on a sunny day that just zaps the ants. That is what He could do. But we see in Revelation that God struggles to bring Himself to this conclusion. It all plays out over time because God is patient and He loves. No. Love will not allow God to merely "zap" creation. God loves and He has given us a drama to be caught up in so that we of our own free-will, will chose to be a Lion-Lamb-Lover. He rescued us from this dilemma of rebellion and universal revolt. Without this story of human deeds and decisions weighed in the balance of God's judgment, human life spirals downward. Judgment gives all men the assurance that evil will receive its just desserts. It also teaches us that hell is a monument to free-will; we can be successful rebels to the very end if we want, but God will not allow rebellion in his good creation anymore.

The sense I get is that if mankind will turn to God; if Earth Dwellers would all repent and welcome God back into the world, then God could intervene and stop the carnage in Revelation. But hearts will be so hard, that they will refuse to do so and Revelation is about how hard their hearts will be. God created you with free will. He will not override you. He will honor it to the very end and hell is a monument to free will. "I will not make you love me," God says. "I will not meticulously control your every move." "You can accept or reject my love, but my broad purposes of restoration will move forward for all Lion Lamb lovers. Your refusal will not be allowed to sabotage my creation."

God does not walk away from creation but invites Earth Dwellers to repent clear up until the very end. He even gets creative and lets us see what life is like without Him. And He does not stand idly by and watch the mayhem. He takes steps to redeem. And yet, He honors free will, "You can have it if you want it," and He steps back and lets you rebel and reveal who you truly are. God lets Himself be pushed out of your life and out of the world and on to the Cross. But the time will come when all free will decisions will be called into account.

10 A FRAMING STORY

In J. R. R. Tolkien's *Lord of the Rings*, Sam says to Frodo Baggins: "I wonder what sort of tale we've fallen into?"[26] I believe this is the question of our time. The world has lost its story. We do not see a drama playing out on a grand scale.

Metanarrative

It is important to talk about framing stories, about meta-narratives, about larger, bigger picture things. Revelation is a framing story. A framing story tells us who we are, where we came from, what went wrong in the world, and where it is all headed, and what we are going to do about it. We are born into this world and unless we know the larger, framing story, we have no idea what part we are to play, how we are to respond to life, and what we are to give ourselves to.

It is like we have showed up at the movie too late and we cannot make sense of the characters, the plot, nor the conversations. Confused and scratching our heads, we settle for lesser stories to star in – little stories to live for – an affair, a

---

[26] Tolkien, J. R. R., *The Lord of the Rings: 50th Anniversary Addition*, (Boston: Houghton Mifflin Company, 2004), pp. 711-712.

better office at work, a few more dollars, a little more control and power, a quick buzz, a little more fame. We miss this grand story that is playing out as presented in Revelation.

What is Your Framing Story?

Revelation is your framing story. If you miss this story, you will never get life right. God has given us the ultimate framing story that supersedes and replaces our little mini-framing stories.[27]

Some people live in a framing story that weaves together all the grievances of life that need to be avenged. Their whole story is defined by the time when they can get even with the former spouse, the co-worker, or the family member. They will never forgive and live in grace. Others have a framing story of superiority and explain why one group or party should have dominance over another group. They will never seek reconciliation with anyone because pride will not allow it. Others have a framing story of moral freedom, that there is no reason to live life with limits or moral constraints. Many have a framing story that says, "I have a limited number of minutes in my short life and I'm going to consume all I can before it's over." Many have a framing story that says "Humans are a mass of atoms with no higher value to the story of life." We are just "overbuilt banana-pickers"[28] to use a phrase from a favorite author of mine.

There are a lot of bad stories in the world, but in Revelation, we have a great story that frames the bad ones. You bring your bad story, your addiction story to the Lion Lamb and when you

---

[27] McLaren, Brian, *Everything Must Change: Jesus, Global Crises, and a Revolution of Hope*, (Nashville: Thomas Nelson, 2007), pp. 67-80.

[28] Cosgrove, Mark P., *Foundations of Christian Thought: Faith, Learning, and the Christian Worldview*, (Grand Rapids: Kregal, 2006).

nest it in His story, you see the power of evil broken. The Lion Lamb walks among us and He lives in the hearts of those loyal to Him. He wants you to situate your story into another story – a story that says that the Earth Maker and Throne Sitter are good and that the Dragon (World Hater) is the true villain. The Lion Lamb wins a place for all Earth Dwellers around his table and we are meant to rule from an appointed throne someday if we will but accept the invitation.

The Lion Lamb gives us a framing story that says we are made in God's image and therefore, we are contended for and fought for against the powers of evil. The story of the Lion Lamb is that He is worthy to open the scroll and lay claim to the title-deed of this planet (Revelation 5), that no demonic army or force will win (Revelation 9), and that no Earth Dweller will be big enough to keep God from breaking into our world.

Twenty-Two Chapters – God is Patient

God made the world good, but we Earth Dwellers messed it up. We are made free-will creatures by a self-limited God who lovingly allows us to co-create our future with Him or against Him. That is why it takes twenty-two chapters to get it all communicated in Revelation. If God did not love humankind, it would all be over in a flash. But He does love us and works with us and the decisions we make. God does not want to see people destroy their lives, so He works with them over time to woo them home. God wants to save humanity and heal it, but in rebellion, we just spiral downward and downward, and yet God keeps pursuing.

In Jesus' framing story, we see that God sent Him as a Rescuer. And if we will surrender to the Rescuer, we can participate in the transformation of the world. We see in Revelation, that it is important to pursue virtue and values because they play large in the larger battle that is being waged on this planet; that we either align ourselves with the Lion

Lamb or with the Beasts and Earth Dwellers who have barricaded themselves in to keep God out; that every act, every decision, every attitude plays into the larger story of restoration or the story of decay. I either reflect God's glory or I tarnish it. I either live for the New Jerusalem or for Babylon. I either rendezvous with the Harlot or save myself for the Bride-Groom. I either follow the Lion Lamb or I live as an Earth Dweller here and now. That is why this story was addressed to the churches. It is John's *magnum opus* to them so that they might be loyal to the Kingdom. They understood the framing story.

When you were born, you landed in the middle of a larger story – a God-sized story. Rather than hijacking the story of God and turning it into a story of "us" like Earth Dwellers do in Revelation, let us surrender to it. It is a universal story of redemption that makes a claim on everybody and calls for a decision. You have been redeemed, purchased by God. You belong to him. Grace has already happened for you in and through Jesus. Your name has been written in the Book of Life. Your job is to believe the Lion Lamb and live differently and be renewed and refuse to go in life directions that says, "I don't care if He blots my name out of some book."

Is It Possible to Change?

Elie Wiesel, the concentration camp survivor, said: "God made man because he loves stories." I like that. But I want to modify Wiesel's statement. Here is how I would say it: "God made man *with free will* because he loves stories *with surprise endings*." You have the capacity to surprise and delight God with the decisions that you make. He is watching your story and has been for a long time.

Maybe you are wondering, "Can I really change? I have been an Earth Dweller all my life." I am reminded of a great point that Clark Pinnock made in one of his books using the story of Ebenezer Scrooge. We all know the story of Ebenezer Scrooge.

After Scrooge saw his life with help from the various spirits and realized the direction of his life (even seeing his own tombstone), he finally woke up and realized that only a few hours had passed in real time, and that it was all a vision. In reference to the tombstone which Scrooge saw in the vision, he asks: "Are these the shadows of the things that will be, or are they the shadows of the things that may be, only?" He adds: "Men's course will foreshadow certain ends to which, if persevered in, they must lead, but if the courses be departed from, the ends will change.' So he pleads, "Assure me that I may yet change these shadows you have shown me, by an altered life. Oh, tell me that I may sponge away the writing on this stone." Clark Pinnock observes: "Scrooge wanted to know if the future was still being shaped and, if so, whether his actions could affect it."[29] Scrooge wanted an opportunity to change! He saw where his life was headed and wanted to redirect it once he discovered that he really was able to.

In a way, I have showed you "shadows" of things to come. John has caught us all up in a visionary story. We have begun to see God's eternal plan play out in vivid detail. We have even seen our demise if we persist in the Earth Dwelling cause. And now, today, it is as if we can wake up from this grand vision that we have been in and realize that we still have time; that we can alter the course of our lives; that we have a place in God's story of redemption. Scrooge pleads over the tombstone, "Assure me that I may yet change these shadows you have shown me, by an altered life. Oh, tell me that I may sponge away the writing on this stone." You can change, and that's why we have this book.

A Life Trajectory is Set

---

[29] Pinnock, Clark, *Most Moved Mover: A Theology of God's Openness*, (Grand Rapids: Baker Academic, 2001), p. 137.

There is a verse in the last chapter of Revelation that might lead you to think differently.

Revelation 22:11 says:

> "Let him who does wrong continue to do wrong; let him who is vile continue to be vile; let him who does right continue to do right; and let him who is holy continue to be holy."

John simply states that after encountering the high impact teaching of this book, some people will make a decision to pursue a life trajectory of non-repentance. Some will choose to follow the Dragon and be an Earth Dweller, living for the world only. The further you go into the Day of the Lord, the harder your heart becomes. Some will choose to be loyal to the Lion Lamb and will become a City Dweller in the New Jerusalem. As the Day of the Lord draws near and God seeks to woo and win hearts, minds will be made up. After all cycles of judgment have run their course, some people will remain unchanged. If they have persisted in their rebellion, by the time you get to the end of all this, then no major changes in an Earth Dweller's conduct should be expected now. Their minds have been made up. The longer you go into a life trajectory, the harder it is to change. This verse is not suggesting that God does not want Earth Dwellers to repent. Rather, it is saying that they will not repent, and John simply says, "May they be allowed to persist in their rebellion because that is how a God of love works."

Puppet Strings

Randy Rowland wrote an intriguing book several years ago called *The Sins We Love*. He tells about singer-songwriter Randy Stonehill, who in the late 70's, early 80's, portrayed rebellion as a puppet (or marionette) who, hoping to be free, cuts its own strings. The song is called "Puppet Strings." The point of the song is not that we are mere puppets moved by some Divine Deity. Rather, we are dependent on a Life Giver but have decided to cut our ties with Him. Say's Rowland of the puppets: "We all know that such action does not result in freedom – rather it leaves just a pile on the floor." [30] Like the puppets who reach up and cut the strings that enable and direct them, we lay crumpled and broken on the stage of life. Rebellion is like that. Rebellion does not want to be dependent on anyone, but superior to everyone, and accountable to no one. We have reached up and cut the strings.

I had a guy who heard me use Rowland's illustration in a talk that I gave and he actually traced the song down. Here are the lyrics and the song that I would like to close this book with. I think it captures best my own heart and emotions.

> I can't keep from mourning for this topsy-turvy world / With all its strife and pain / Mourning for the lost and the desperate children / Who can't remember their names
>
> And I can feel it in my soul / Now the end is getting near / I can hear the devil laughing / And its ringing in my ears
>
> Long ago He chose us to inherit all His kingdom / And we were blessed with light/ But wandering away we disobeyed Him in the garden / And stumbled into night

---

[30] Rowland, Randy, *The Sins We Love*, (Doubleday: New York, New York, 2000), 15.

> And I can feel it in my soul / Now the end is getting near / I can hear the angels weeping / And it's ringing in my ears
>
> We are all like foolish puppets who desiring to be kings / Now lie pitifully crippled after cutting our own strings
>
> But God said I'll forgive you I will face you Man to man / And win your love again / Oh how could there be possibly a greater gift of love / Than dying for a friend
>
> And I can feel it in my soul / Now the end is getting near / I can hear the devil laughing / And it's ringing in my ears
>
> We are all like foolish puppets who desiring to be kings / Now lie pitifully crippled after cutting our own strings
>
> Cutting our own strings / Cutting our own strings / Cutting our own strings[31]

We have all "cut our strings." But all Earth Dwellers who are willing, can come to the Lion Lamb and swear allegiance to Him. He repairs the broken strings and reconnects us with the Throne Sitter again.

---

[31] Randy Stonehill, author. Lyrics available at and last accessed, August 2011: http://www.justsomelyrics.com/2248257/Randy-Stonehill-Puppet-Strings-Lyrics

Appendix One

Sequence of Events in the Book of Revelation

Revelation 1:1-3:22

Letters to the Churches in the First Century

These letters are applicable to all churches in the church age.

Revelation 4:1-19:21

The Tribulational Period to Come

Many see this as a seven year period of time.

Revelation 20:1-10

The Millennial Reign of Christ

This is the one-thousand year reign of Christ on earth.

Revelation 20:11-22:21

Judgment and Eternity

This describes life as it will be in the eternal state.

Appendix Two

Key Character Identification in the Book of Revelation

The Lion Lamb – Jesus Christ (1;4; 5)

The Throne Sitter – God (5:1)

Great Multitude – Martyred Saints (7:9)

Elders – Church Leaders in Heaven (7:11)

A Woman Clothed with the Sun – Israel (12:1-2)

The Red Dragon with Seven Heads and Ten Horns – Satan (12:3-4)

The Male Child – Christ (12:5-6)

Archangel Casting Satan Out of Heaven – Michael (12:7-12)

Woman's Offspring – Israel (12:13-17)

The Beast Out of the Sea – Future World Dictator (13:2-10)

The Beast Out of the Earth – False Prophet (13:11-18)

144,000 – Tribes of Israel (14)

The Harlot – Quasi-Religious and Political Entity (17, 18)

The Saints – Lion Lamb Followers

City Dwellers – Residents of the New Jerusalem

Appendix Three

I love the overview of Revelation presented by Gordon D. Fee and Douglas Stuart. Here is the way this book moves according to Fee and Stuart.[32] It unfolds like a great drama. In the early scenes or chapters, we meet a cast of characters and the latter scenes involving these characters are dependent on the early scenes.

Chapters 1-6 set the stage for the drama, "starting with a vision of the risen Christ who holds the keys to everything that follows."[33]

John addresses some specific churches in *Revelation 2-3*. These were literal churches that existed at the time of John's writing.

In *Revelation 4-5*, there is a vision of the Creator God and the Redeeming Lamb, before whom all will bow. "John weeps because no one can be found to break the seals of the scroll (which is full of God's justice and righteous judgments)." But John is told that "the Lion of the tribe of Judah, the "Root of David" has triumphed (Revelation 5). And yet this worthy One is perplexing to John because all he can see is a slain Lamb.

---

[32] Fee, Gordon and Stuart, Douglas, *How to Read Bible Book by Book: A Guided Tour*, (Grand Rapids: Zondervan, 2002), pp. 426-436.

[33] Ibid, p. 434.

Nevertheless, the Lion-Lamb set's the drama in motion by breaking the seals (6). These seal judgments provide an overture for what follows (conquest, war, famine, death). These are followed by martyrdoms (seal 5), to which God responds with judgment (seal 6).

In *Revelation 7*, there are two interlude visions between judgments which deal with those whom God has sealed from harm.

In *Revelation 8-9*, we read of more judgments which "echo the plagues of Egypt against their present-day Pharaoh"[34] say Fee and Stuart. And just as in Pharaoh's day, the plagues do not lead to repentance (*9:20-21*), so it will be in John's time and beyond, with mankind sticking with their rebellion no matter what.

There is another interlude vision between the sixth and seventh trumpets that calls for the current Christ followers on earth to bear a faithful witness (*chapters 10-11*).

The remaining visions in Revelation (*chapters 12-22*) "offer explanations for and apocalyptic descriptions of the final doom of the empire."[35]

Chapter 12 is the theological key to the book. In two visions we are told of Satan's attempt to destroy Christ and of his own defeat instead. Satan is revealed as a defeated foe whose end has not come yet. And there is woe pronounced over the world because Satan's time is limited and he is taking vengeance. The

---

[34] Ibid, p. 435.

[35] Ibid, p. 435.

anti-God Empire of Rome is doomed and its destruction is portrayed in the seven bowl judgments (*chapters 12-16*).

Two cities are set against each other – Rome and Jerusalem. Like two women, one portrayed as a prostitute and one portrayed as the Bride of the Lamb or Wife of Yahweh, they rise up to face each other in battle against the backdrop of God's final salvation and judgment (*chapters 17-20*).

Of course, the Bride of Christ prevails and gets to dance with the King in a palace called New Jerusalem on a high mountain (*chapters 21-22*) while Babylon, the Harlot, perched on the back of the Beast, is destroyed in the desert. Christ takes on the Beast and conquers the barbarian hordes. The Beast (the Anti-God world system), the Harlot on the Beast (the World Ruler), and the false prophet are one-by-one thrown into the Lake of Fire (*19:20; 20:10*).

ABOUT THE AUTHOR

Joey Nelson is a pastor in Indiana. He holds a Bachelor's and Master's degree in Biblical Studies. He has pastored for over eighteen years.

You may order copies of this book.
Simply search for the *book title* or *author's name* at:
www.amazon.com

If you have comments or questions or would like to order an autographed copy of this book directly from the author, you may send an email to Joey Nelson at:
lionlambfollower@yahoo.com

Made in the USA
Middletown, DE
10 April 2022